All About POOP

Written by:
Kate Hayes

Illustrated by:
Brenna Vaughan

Published by Pinwheel Books

Brookline, MA

www.pinwheelbooks.com

ISBN 978-0-985-4248-00

Library of Congress Control Number: 2012906114

Printed in China

For Tobey and Ava
B.V.

For Kellen, Anna, and Kyle,
who make every day a wonderful adventure!
K.H.

Have you ever wondered all about poop?

Why our bodies make such stinky goop?

And where does it go after we wipe

when the poop is flushed down through a pipe?

I can tell you, but first, how rude!
Pardon me, I'll swallow my food!
Speaking of food, that's where it starts—
poop, I mean (and also farts).

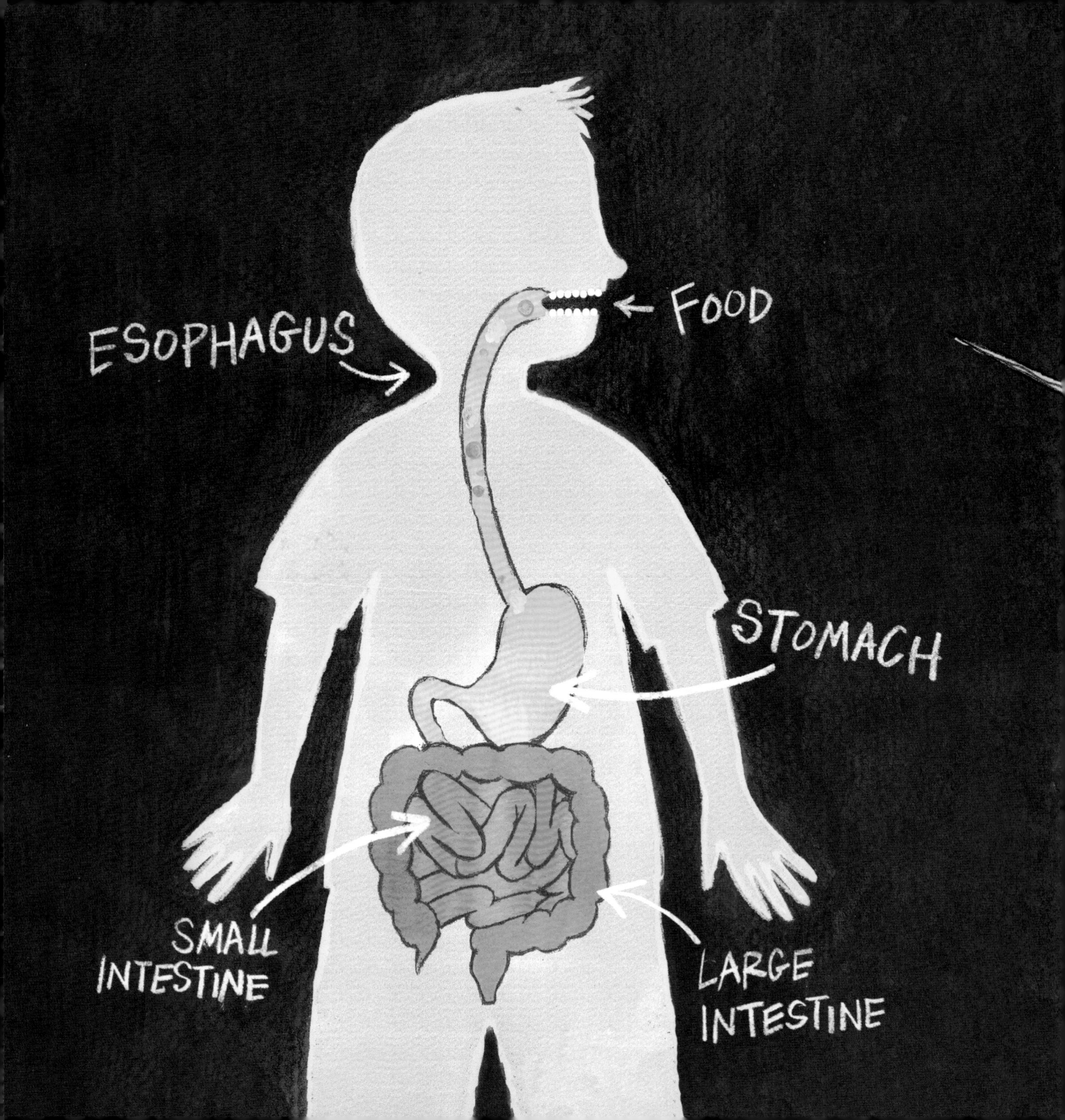

ESOPHAGUS

FOOD

STOMACH

SMALL INTESTINE

LARGE INTESTINE

You chew up your food, and then you swallow,
and the pieces go into a tube that's hollow.
The tube takes the food into your tummy.
Then what happens is not quite so yummy.

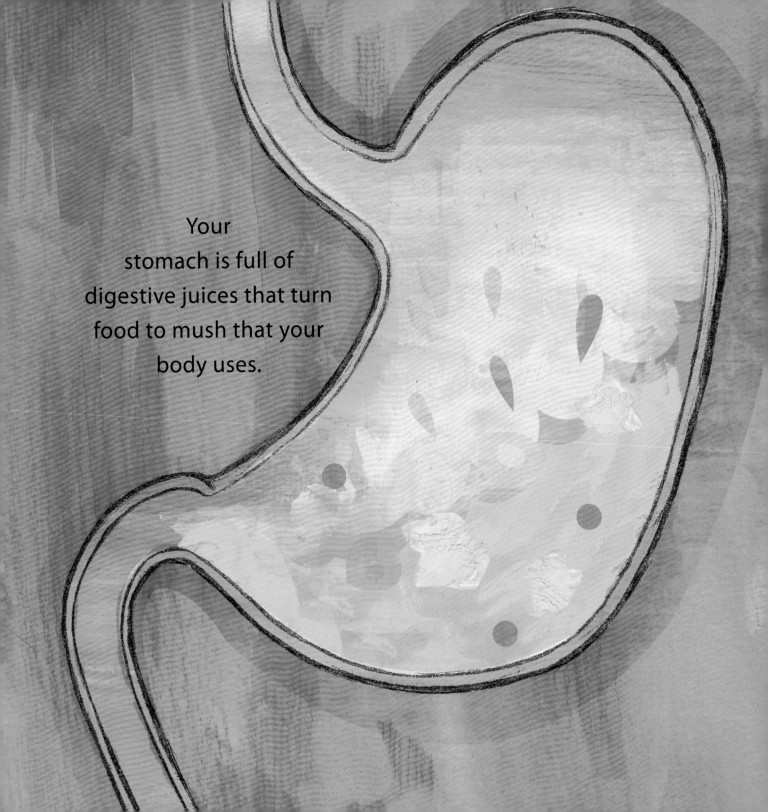

Your stomach is full of digestive juices that turn food to mush that your body uses.

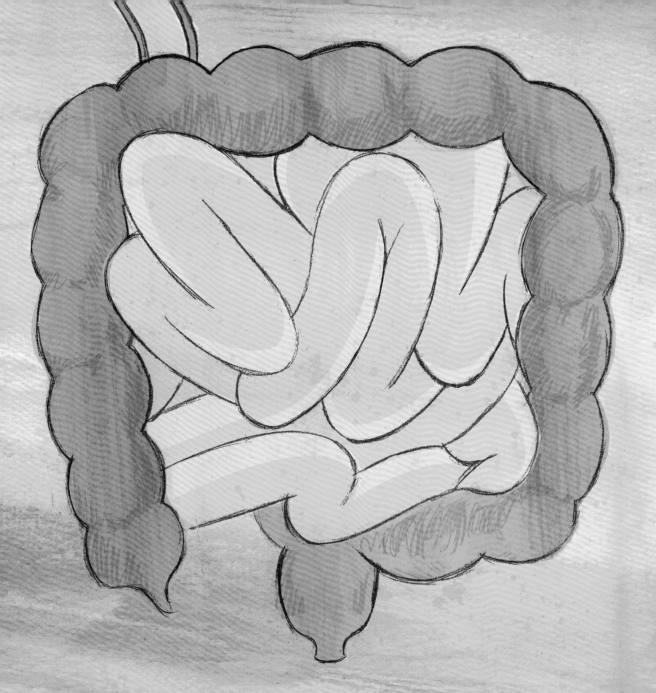

Into your intestines the mushy food goes.
Intestines are like a long snake or a hose.

The small intestine sucks nutrients out of your food.
(That's the healthy stuff, as you might conclude.)

The large intestine slurps all the water away
till it looks less like mush and more like brown clay.

What you have left is a nice solid lump
of your body's own waste,

LIKE TRASH FOR THE DUMP!

Sometimes your intestines create smelly gas,

which sneaks out in the farts or the toots that you pass. (Excuse me!)

Toots can be signals that help you to know
it's time to run to the bathroom and go!

You sit and you push till you hear a

plop
ploop!

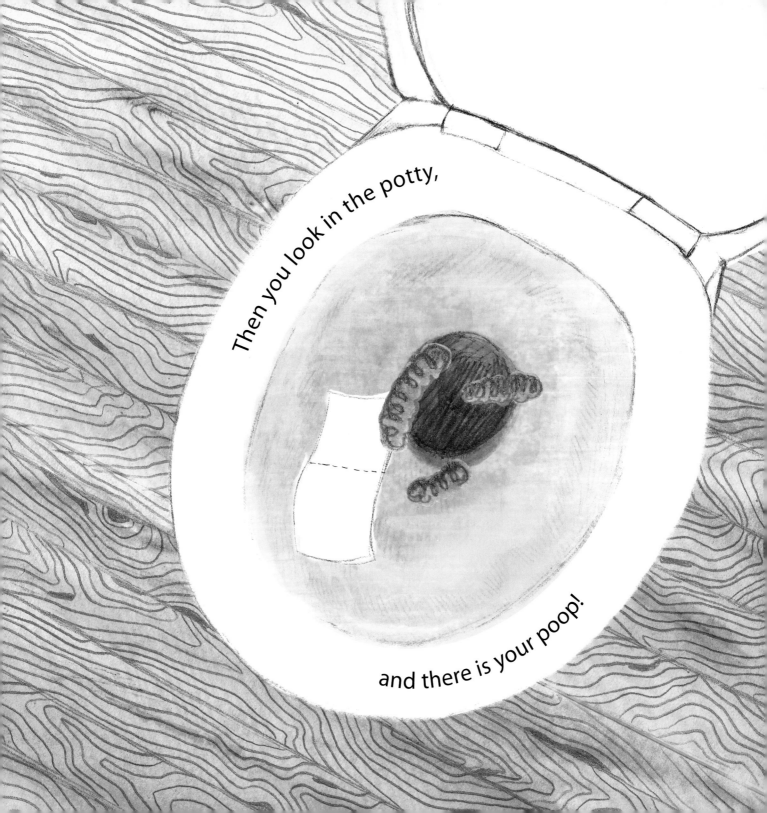

Then you look in the potty, and there is your poop!

There are so many different names for poo,
like "doo-doo" or "caca" or "toilet bowl stew."
Our teacher calls poop "number two" at my school.
My dad calls it...

Dropping the kids at the pool!

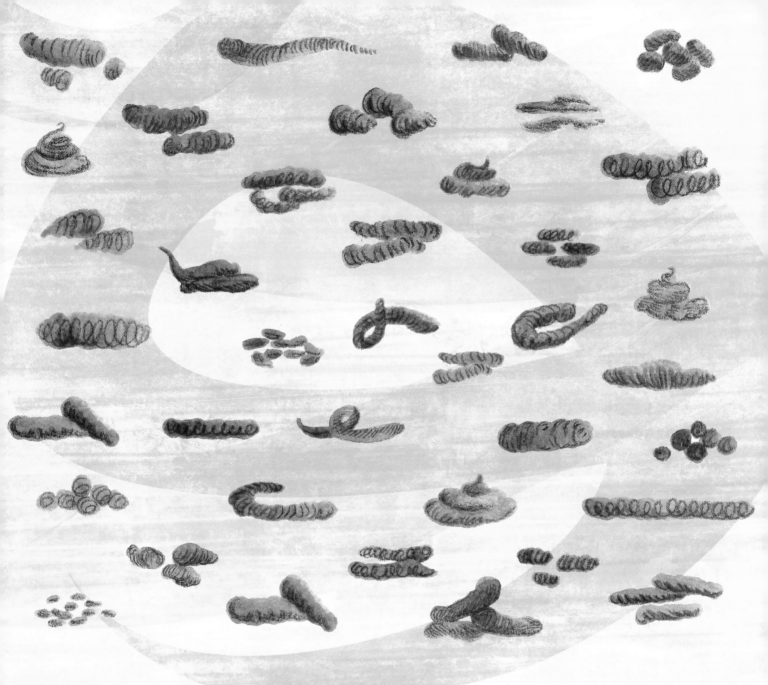

Poop comes in a mixture of all shapes and sizes.
There are so many possible poop surprises!

Some poop floats and some poop sinks.
One thing that's for sure is that
ALL POOP STINKS!
(PEE-EW!)

To get rid of the poop (and the smell) you must flush.
Push the handle till the water comes down with a rush.
It swirls the poop 'round and it's whisked away
down into the pipes, like a swift poop ballet!

The pipes take the poop right out of the room,
then out of the house through an underground flume.
From there it goes into a septic tank,
along with the pee from the water you drank.

Other pipes take our waste to a sewage plant,
a place that cleans poop in ways that we can't.

Boy, am I glad poop's got somewhere to go!
I wouldn't like to keep it in here,
you know?

Oh, and one more thing that you need to learn...

...You can't touch poop 'cause poop has germs!

Germs can make people really sick,
so after you poop you should wash
your hands quick!

Now, if you don't mind, I'll go back to my soup.

My job here is done...
You know all about poop!

5 things

TO REMEMBER

about

POOP

1. **NEVER** touch poop with your hands.
2. Don't ~~poop~~ in your pants - - -
   ALWAYS USE THE POTTY!
3. Wipe your bottom
   when you're done pooping
4. (FRONT TO → BACK)
   Always **WASH** your hands
   after you poop
   [you can also use hand sanitizer]
5. IT'S NOT NICE to TALK ABOUT POOP UNLESS
   • you're telling someone you need
   to use the bathroom...
   OR • reading **this** book
   DON'T BE A POTTY MOUTH!

Did You Know?

Cockroaches toot every 15 minutes!

:45
:30
:15

Hello.

HERRING (A TYPE OF FISH) USE FARTS TO COMMUNICATE WITH EACH OTHER.

So NICE TO SEE YOU.

Cats like to BURY THEIR POOP.
(SO DO ARMADILLOS AND WOODCHUCKS)

One chore of American pioneer children was to gather buffalo poop, or "buffalo chips," to use as fuel to burn in fires.

An adult African Elephant can produce up to 300 pounds of poop each day!

Your poop weighs more than my parents!

Pinwheel Books
www.pinwheelbooks.com

Kate Hayes is a professional writer, nationally recognized mom blogger, and former TV news journalist. By day, she works as a B2B marketing content developer and social media strategist. By night, she writes about the joys and struggles of being a working mom on her blog, Adventures in Parenting (www.adventuresinparenting.me). Kate was named one of the BlogHer Voices of the Year in 2011 and was a Scholastic Parent & Child Magazine Parent Blogger Award winner in 2010. She lives with her husband and two kids in the Boston area. To learn more about Kate, visit her website at www.authorkatehayes.com or connect with her on Twitter: @bostonblogmom.

Brenna Vaughan has a BFA in illustration from Memphis College of Art. She works in a blend of digital and traditional media combining watercolor, acrylic and ink with digital techniques. She lives in St. Louis, MO with her husband and two children. This is Brenna's first children's book. To see her illustrations, visit www.brennaillustration.com.

To download our free **All About Poop Teacher and Parent Guide,** produced in collaboration with **Hooked on Science,** go to www.facebook.com/allaboutpoop.